A Child's
Book of Manners

Helen Oxenbury
and Fay Maschler

Jonathan Cape Thirty Bedford Square London

First published 1978
Illustrations © 1978 by Helen Oxenbury
Text © 1978 by Fay Maschler
Jonathan Cape Ltd, 30 Bedford Square, London WC1

British Library Cataloguing in Publication Data

Oxenbury, Helen
  A child's book of manners.
  1. Etiquette for children and youth
  I. Title   II. Maschler, Fay
  395   BJ1877.C5

ISBN 0 224 01620 2

Printed in Great Britain by
W. S. Cowell Ltd, Butter Market, Ipswich

A cousin of Arty's called Neil
Had been told it was sinful to steal;
But if emptied, his pockets
Showed pen-knives and lockets
And things you would rather not feel.

Kittens, puppies, gerbils, fish
All require caring for:
Though once they were your greatest wish
Now you act like they're a bore.

You leave your mum to get the meal
The rabbits really like,
And while your hamster treads his wheel
You whizz round on your bike.

A pet is not a moving toy
You tire of at your leisure:
For every owner, girl or boy,
There's work as well as pleasure.

Be nice to a new baby,
I know it's not much fun:
She doesn't joke, won't play games
And cannot even run.

She occupies your mother,
Who could be doing things
Like cutting out, or sticking down,
Or pushing you on swings.

Be kind to a new baby,
It might pay off in the end –
For that naggy little bundle
Could turn out to be a friend.

Alice Morris had a voice
That you could hardly hear.
Her parents found it quite beyond
The range of human ear.

She used it when she wanted things,
And then she'd moan "It's mine."
Oh, Alice dear, that weedy noise
Is what we call a whine.

Whining does a funny trick
Of turning inside out,
And stopping people giving you
The thing you're on about.

The thing a parent most dislikes
(Apart from tripping over trikes
And picking Lego up from floors)
Is the noise of slamming doors.
They hate it most at early morning.
So, children, listen to this warning,
And if you roam about the house
Please imitate the docile mouse.

Doors have handles.
Doors have jambs.
What doors should never have
Are slams.

Sometimes, in the afternoon,
Your mother might seek out her room,
And though you'd view it with surprise
There lie down and close her eyes.
Her dreams might also puzzle you;
But see it from her point of view,
And don't upset this little pause
With the noise of banging doors.

Doors have handles.
Doors have jambs.
What doors should never have
Are slams.

Celia always took her time
Over what she had to do.
She'd take at least six minutes
Just to fasten up one shoe.

To find her coat would be a task
Of many minutes more;
It could be half an hour
Before Celia reached the door.

"Please *hurry*" and "Don't *dawdle*"
Meant nothing to that child.
Celia always took her time
To drive her parents wild.

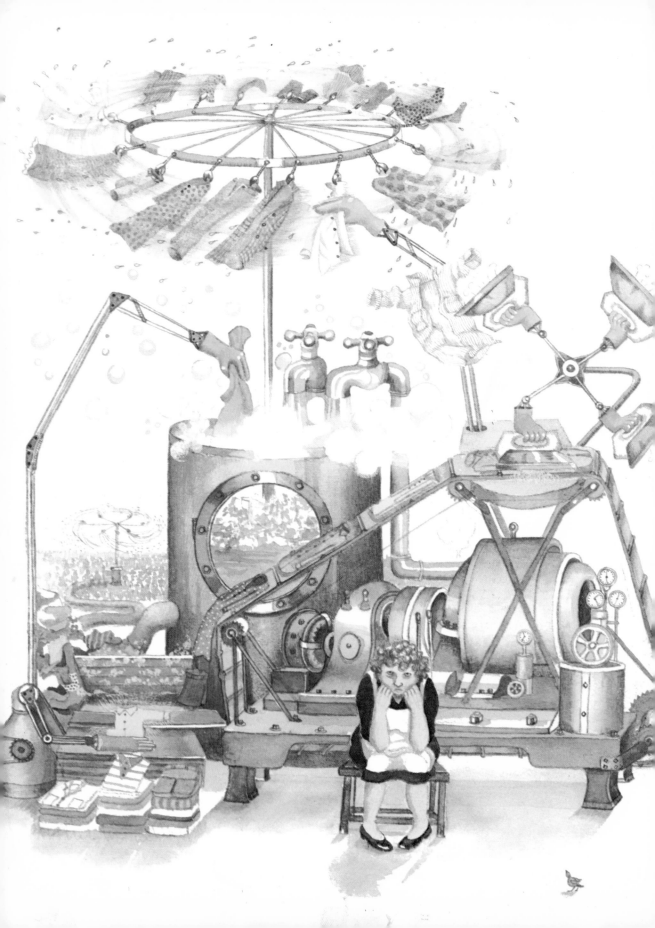

Once there was a child called Ruth
Who very seldom told the truth.
In fact I'm sure some early fibs
Were at the time she still wore bibs.
She'd show her mum she'd scoffed her peas
When ten were tucked behind her knees.
Then as little Ruth grew older
The tales she told got somewhat bolder.
That decoration (felt-tip-penned)
She vowed was done by her best friend,
And asked to find Kate's long lost dolly
Ruth became just frightfully jolly.
Soon family and friends grew wise,
And nodded when Ruth told her lies.
Now here's the sad part of this story
To contemplate if you seek glory:
Ruth produced a great invention . . .
But no one paid the least attention.

Audrey Evans, the most awful fuss-pot,
Was always telling her sisters they must not
Move her dollies or touch her own toys
(Audrey could make the most fearful noise).

Each morning she'd fuss about what to wear:
It got so her mother would almost not dare
To offer this dress or that pair of jeans
(Audrey was known for the strength of her screams).

And mealtimes became a terrible test
Of guessing what Audrey, that day, liked best:
Her father supposed the child would eat leeks
(Others long afterwards spoke of her shrieks).

In the end Audrey's family had to ignore
Her fussing and fretting and being a bore
About what she wanted. They left her alone.
(And Audrey developed a *far* sweeter tone.)

Little Arty at the party
Ate up every single Smartie.
After that I saw him take
The hugest slice of chocolate cake.

His glass he filled with something fizzy;
Then, keeping Jenny's mother busy,
Asked if he could please take back
That jelly just refused by Jack.

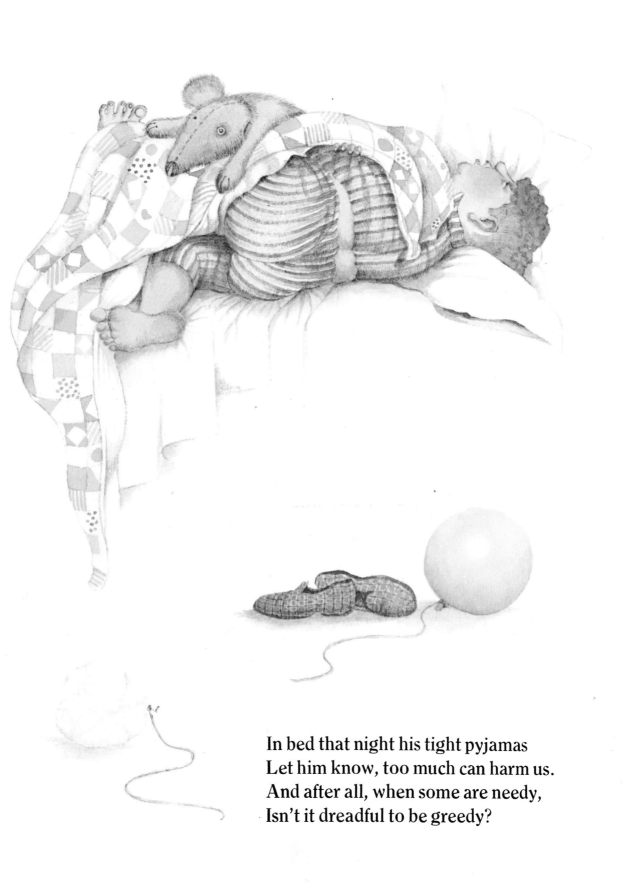

In bed that night his tight pyjamas
Let him know, too much can harm us.
And after all, when some are needy,
Isn't it dreadful to be greedy?

One of the girls at Audrey's school
Would terrify the others.
She'd talk about a Creep that lurks
And of a Thing that smothers.

She'd tell them that she'd be in touch
(Unless they gave her stuff
Like necklaces and sharpeners)
With the beasts that acted rough.

The children were too scared to tell
And never explained fully
About this girl, whom we won't name,
Except to call her bully.

Harriet, Henry and Stan
Ate baked beans straight from the can,
Scorned anything green
And were not to be seen
When their mother prepared them a flan.

Harriet, Henry and Stan
Would lick spoons or clean out a pan
But cook them a meal
And the trio would squeal
"We can't come. You're spoiling our plan."

Harriet, Henry and Stan
Drove their mother (her name was Fran)
To leave them alone;
She talks on the phone.
Now they eat whenever they can.

There's not a lot that you can do
Travelling in a car:
Your parents may promote the view,
Or promise "It's not far,"
But occupying all the seat
Or pinching someone's arm
Or fighting meanly with your feet
Could really do some harm.
The driver has to think about
The road, the lights, that lorry;
And if you shock him with a shout
You might be very sorry.

Little bits of soft-boiled egg
Spread along the table leg
Annoy a parent even more
Than toast and jam dropped on the floor.
(When you're bashing on the ketchup
Keep in mind where it might fetch up.)
Try to keep the food you eat
Off your clothes and off your seat,
On your plate and fork and knife.
This holds true throughout your life.

Games are never so much fun
Once you've lost the bits,
So tidy carefully away
Your jigsaws and your kits.

Dominoes and games like that
Which need to be divided
With too few pieces never let
A winner be decided.

Snakes and Ladders with no dice,
Happy Families missing mothers
Clutter up your shelves and are
Useless to pass on to others.

Mud when you are out of doors
Doesn't show. It shows on floors,
And carpets too, and on the stairs
And, should you put your feet there, chairs.

If you don't want your mum to lose
Her temper, then take off your shoes
Or muddy boots. Then you can race
Around the house and leave no trace.

That witch at the window's a curtain.
A story for teddy's been read.
That you are not thirsty I'm certain —
Please stay the whole night in your bed.